COMBAT AIRCRAFT SERIES

F/A-18 Hornet

LINDSAY PEACOCK

OSPREY PUBLISHING LONDON

Published in 1986 by
Osprey Publishing Ltd
Member Company of the George Philip Group
12–14 Long Acre, London WC2E 9LP

British Library Cataloguing in Publication Data

Peacock, Lindsay T.
    F/A-18 Hornet. — (Osprey combat aircraft)
    1. Hornet (Jet fighter plane) — History
    I. Title
    623.74'64   UG1242.F5

ISBN 0-85045-707-6

Typeset by Flair plan Photo-typesetting Ltd.
Printed by Proost International Book Production,
Turnhout, Belgium.

Colour: profiles page 26-27, © Pilot Press Ltd.;
remainder, Stephen Seymour, Mike Keep, Brian
Knight © Bedford Editions Ltd.
Cutaway drawing: Michael Badrocke
Diagrams: TIGA
Photographs: Supplied by McDonnell Douglas
Corporation, the US Department of Defense and
Canadian Armed Forces.

The Author

LINDSAY PEACOCK turned to aviation journalism
from many years of aircraft "spotting" (which still
takes up much of his time) and photography. He has
written extensively on military aircraft subjects for
books and for magazines, especially in areas of
specific interest to aircraft modellers. He has
travelled widely in pursuit of his hobbies, and spent
much time on aircraft carrier decks observing his
subject at close quarters.

Contents

1
Hornet Evolution

BACK IN the early 1960s, there were many who expressed surprise when the US Navy's McDonnell F4H Phantom was selected by the US Air Force's Tactical Air Command to perform close air support, interdiction and counter air missions. With the benefit of hindsight, the wisdom of this decision is clear, for the Phantom—eventually the F-4 Phantom II—ultimately matured into a quite superlative warplane.

Thirteen years later, the wheel turned full circle when the US Navy opted for the McDonnell Douglas/Northrop F/A-18 Hornet—ironically enough partly to replace the Phantom—although in this instance the USAF had rejected the Hornet's predecessor, the YF-17 which had lost out to the General Dynamics YF-16 in the Air Combat Fighter (ACF) contest of 1974. Thus, although the mid-70s technically marked the start of the F/A-18 programme, the evolution process dates back to events which took place almost a decade earlier.

It was then that Northrop's design bureau—headed by Lee Begin, Jr.—began work on a new concept, although it took time for their ideas to crystallize into a definite proposal. By 1967, however, the P-530 Cobra was beginning to take shape, its

Below: Northrop's YF-17 was an indispensable forerunner to the F/A-18 Hornet. Both of the prototypes of this lightweight fighter are seen here above the Mojave Desert.

origins being readily apparent in that the wing planform was virtually identical to that of the F-5, although it was shoulder-mounted and of greater area with a leading edge extension (LEX) at the root.

Thereafter, the rapid initial progress gave way to a period of apparent official inertia, the next few years being a time of great frustration for Northrop, possibly as a result of having made such a good aircraft in the F-5, a type which was still in great demand. Understandably, this inertia did not extend to Northrop which continued to promote the P-530 while further refining its design.

Small, light fighter requirement

There matters might have stagnated but for two individuals who, in 1971, began to advocate the lightweight fighter concept. One was defence systems analyst Pierre M. Sprey who, while not necessarily in a strong position with regard to influencing procurement, was able to argue the virtues of a low-cost lightweight fighter. The other was Major John Boyd who was serving on the Air Force Prototype Study Group in 1971 and who pushed the radical concept that "small and light is beautiful" very hard. Despite the fact that there were many whose views ran counter to Boyd's, his determination paid off at the beginning of 1972 when the USAF issued a request for proposals (RFP) for a lightweight fighter (LWF).

As far as design was concerned, the contenders were given a fairly free hand, although it was specified that any proposal should possess a minimum design load factor of 6.5g as well as a modest avionics

fit. Low cost was also desirable although, somewhat paradoxically, any new fighter would be expected to employ advanced technology, it being felt that these two aspects were not mutually exclusive.

Boeing, General Dynamics, Ling-Temco-Vought and Northrop all responded, Northrop's candidate being based on the P-600 which was one of several alternatives that emerged in 1971. Eventually, this and the General Dynamics submission were selected for further development, and contracts covering two prototypes of each were awarded on 13 April 1972.

Two years later, the thrust of the LWF programme changed drastically. Previously viewed purely as a technology demonstration exercise, the LWF took on greater significance when it was announced that it would provide the basis for a new Air Combat Fighter (ACF) for the USAF, which was facing up to the reality that it would be unable to purchase sufficient F-15 Eagles. At the bottom line, the Eagle was just too expensive and it was therefore decided to adopt a compromise "hi-lo" mix in which more costly fighters operated in conjunction with less sophisticated and commensurately less expensive machines. Rather than develop a new ACF from scratch, the LWF project seemed to offer the best chance of "cutting corners" and obtaining the "low-cost" portion quickly, hence its elevation in status.

It was against this background that the first YF-17 (72-01569) was rolled-out at Hawthorne, California,

Above: Resplendent in blue, white and gold trim, the first of nine full-scale development (FSD) F-18As, Bu.No.160775, is portrayed at St Louis, Missouri, shortly after being rolled out. Note the Sidewinder and Sparrow missiles.

on 4 April 1974, this being taken by road to Edwards Air Force Base (AFB) where it flew for the first time on 9 June. It was duly followed by the second prototype (72-01570) which made its maiden flight on 21 August, and these two aircraft were initially employed to accomplish an accelerated test programme before being pitted against the YF-16. During flight testing, the YF-17 generally performed well; it is probably not widely known that it became the first turbojet-powered US type to exceed Mach 1.0 in level flight without afterburner, an event it accomplished on 11 June 1974.

Meeting the Navy's needs

However, the YF-16 was adjudged the winner and ordered in large quantities by the USAF. What is perhaps not so obvious is that the outcome was close-run, with Northrop's contender demonstrating remarkable handling qualities and emerging superior in certain areas. Nevertheless, the USAF felt the F-16 Fighting Falcon was best able to move from technology demonstrator to production fighter. The YF-17 saga might have ended there, had it not been for the US Navy's desire to obtain a new fighter.

Once again, high cost—this time of the F-14A Tomcat—seems to have been influential in prompting the Navy to look for a less expensive type. The Navy's concern in fact dated back to about 1971, but

initial studies failed to obtain full support, those responsible for fighter policy having evolved a new requirement for a fighter possessing secondary attack capability, this being known as the fighter-attack experimental (VFAX). Not unnaturally, the Navy wanted a new design altogether and would probably have proceeded along those lines had it not been for a Congressional directive that they should take a close look at the USAF's ACF contenders. This dictat probably didn't go down too well in the light of an earlier unfortunate experience with the General Dynamics/Grumman F-111B. Nevertheless, in late August 1974, the VFAX operational requirements were issued. Northrop teamed with McDonnell Douglas to promote the YF-17 while General Dynamics joined with Ling-Temco-Vought to meet the demand.

Although both groups had appropriate aircraft flying, evaluation of the two contenders was primarily a paper exercise which ended on 2 May 1975 when the Navy selected McDonnell Douglas/Northrop's F/A-18.

Influential factors

Several factors influenced their decision. For a start, the McDonnell Douglas/Northrop proposal, being twin-engined, would be better suited to operations at sea. Less obvious was the question of multi-mission capability and it was felt that the YF-17 possessed greater potential in this respect, especially because the Navy wished eventually to replace both the F-4 Phantom and A-7 Corsair. Another very important consideration was that of the mechanics involved in operating from an aircraft carrier. The YF-17 advanced the cause of the F/A-18 in this area by demonstrating superior recovery performance in a series of comparative trials against its old protagonist, the YF-16.

However, McDonnell Douglas and Northrop still had a long way to go to transform the YF-17 into a machine capable of enduring the stresses and strains inherent in carrier operations. Meeting this requirement was to be accompanied by constant growth in terms of weight, size and cost. Many of the changes made at this time arose out of the Navy requirements while others were spawned by the process of navalization.

All-weather avionics needed

For instance, the Navy specified compatibility with the AIM-7F Sparrow which requires all-weather avionics and a sophisticated fire control system. In addition, dual fighter/strike missions dictated an increase in fuel capacity so as to provide the necessary endurance, while a considerable amount of structural strengthening was also undertaken. This and other changes prompted the adoption of more powerful engines and an increase in wing area so as to reduce wing loading.

Because it was always intended that the F-18 would be a single-seater, much attention was paid to reducing the work-load on the pilot. Accordingly, the Hornet features the hands on throttle and stick (HOTAS) philosophy which involves those controls required for combat all being located on either the throttle lever or control column. As far as mission-related data is concerned, cathode ray tubes (CRTs) are extensively used, the cockpit being dominated by three of these and associated function control switches. The F-18 also has the now obligatory head-up display (HUD).

All of these revisions added greatly to unit cost and the F-18 is much more expensive than had first been hoped. Of course, coming up with one type to fulfil two or more missions does mean that a long production run is assured which reduces the cost per unit. Nevertheless, the Hornet isn't cheap and the fact that whatever money is available has to be spread thinly means that long service life is essential. In the case of the F-18, the type is designed for a service life of 6,000 flying hours.

Contract awarded

Although selected by the Navy in May 1975, the process of redesign kept both companies busy for the rest of the year and it was not until 22 January 1976 that McDonnell Douglas received a written contract ordering an initial batch of 11 aircraft for full-scale development (FSD) testing. Nine of these aircraft would be completed as single-seat F-18As while the other two would be two-seat TF-18As, and the maiden flight of the first aircraft was set for July 1978.

Even though nearly three years were to elapse before the first Hornet flight, the programme was making headway. The Navy at least had some hardware to play with; the second YF-17 acquiring Navy insignia for test duties with the Pacific Missile Test Center at Point Mugu, California, the Naval Air Test Center at Patuxent River, Maryland, and the Naval Weapons Center at China Lake, California.

Below: Featuring a similar colour scheme to that worn by the initial Hornet, the first two-seat TF-18A streams fuel from the tail dump vents during an early test flight.

2
Structure and Systems

FROM THE viewpoint of design and structure, the Hornet seems to represent a sort of "half-way house". Thus, although it embodies many of the recent advances in fighter design as well as composite materials, most aspects of the basic airframe are well proven.

As part of the agreement between McDonnell Douglas and Northrop, it was decided that fabrication of the baseline F-18 would be split roughly 60/40 between McDonnell Douglas and Northrop, respectively; whereas, in the event of orders being secured for the land-based F-18L, these proportions would be reversed. In broad terms, then, Northrop contributes the centre and aft fuselage sections as well as both vertical fins. These major sub-assemblies are shipped to St Louis, Missouri, where they are mated to the McDonnell Douglas contribution, which comprises the wings, horizontal tail and the foward fuselage including the cockpit.

As far as materials are concerned, just under half—49.6 per cent to be precise—of the structural weight is made up of aluminium, while steel contributes some 16.7 per cent by weight. Titanium adds a further 12.9 per cent, most notably for wing, fin and horizontal tail attachment as well as wing-fold joints. Even though it is employed to cover close to 40 per cent of the surface area, the incredibly strong and corrosion resistant advanced graphite/epoxy composite material accounts for just 9.9 per cent of the weight, the remaining 10.9 per cent being made up of other materials.

Looking beneath the skin, the fuselage is basically a semi-monocoque structure and the three major sections are largely fabricated from light alloy with machined aluminium fuselage frames, Titanium

Below: The Hornet's unique leading edge extensions and twin vertical tails are readily apparent in this fine study of a VMFA-323 machine entering a vortex-inducing turn.

McDONNELL DOUGLAS F/A-18 HORNET CUTAWAY

1. Radome.
2. Planar array radar scanner.
3. Flight refuelling probe, retracable.
4. Gun gas purging air intakes.
5. Radar module withdrawal rails.
6. M61A1 Vulcan 20mm rotary cannon.
7. Ammunition magazine.
8. Angle of attack transmitter.
9. Hinged windscreen (access to instruments).
10. Instrument panel and cathode ray tube displays.
11. Head-up display
12. Engine throttle levers.
13. Martin-Baker Mk 10L 'zero-zero'.
14. Canopy.
15. Cockpit pressurization valve.
16. Canopy actuator.
17. Structural space provision for second seat (TF-18 trainer variant).
18. ASQ-137 Laser Spot Tracker.
19. Wing root leading edge extension (LEX).
20. Position light.
21. Tacan antenna.
22. Intake ramp bleed air spill duct.
23. Starboard wing stores pylons.
24. Leading edge flap.
25. Starboard wing integral fuel tank.
26. Wing fold hinge joint.
27. AIM-9P Sidewinder air-to-air missile.
28. Missile launch rail.
29. Starboard navigation light.
30. Wing tip folded position.
31. Flap vane.

32. Leading edge flap drive shaft interconnection.
33. Starboard drooping aileron.
34. UHF/IFF antenna.
35. Boundary layer bleed air spill duct.
36. Leading edge flap drive motor and gearbox.
37. Engine bleed air ducting.
38. Aft fuselage fuel tanks.
39. Hydraulic reservoirs.
40. Fuel system vent pipe.
41. Fuel venting air grilles.
42. Strobe light.
43. Tail navigation light.
44. Aft radar warning antenna.
45. Fuel jettison.
46. Starboard rudder.
47. Radar warning power amplifier.
48. Rubber hydraulic actuator.
49. Starboard all-moving tailplane.
50. Airbrake.
51. ECM antenna.
52. Radar warning antenna.
53. Formation lighting strip.
54. Variable area afterburner nozzles.
55. Afterburner duct.
56. Engine fire suppression bottles.
57. Arrester hook jack and damper.
58. Port all-moving tailplane.
59. Afterburner nozzle actuator.
60. Tailplane pivot bearing.
61. Arrester hook.
62. Tailplane hydraulic actuator.
63. General Electric F404 afterburning turbofan engine.
64. Engine digital control unit.

65. Formation lighting strip.
66. Engine fuel system equipment.
67. Port drooping aileron.
68. Single slotted Fowler-type flap.
69. Aileron hydraulic actuator.
70. Wing fold rotary actuator and gearbox.
71. Port navigation light.
72. AIM-9P Sidewinder air-to-air missile.
73. Leading edge flap rotary actuator.

74. Port leading edge flap.
75. Airframe mounted engine accessory gearbox, shaft driven.
76. Leading edge slat drive shaft.
77. Auxiliary power turbine.
78. Flap hydraulic jack.
79. Twin stores carrier.
80. Outboard stores pylon.
81. Aft retracting mainwheel.
82. Mk 83 general purpose bombs.

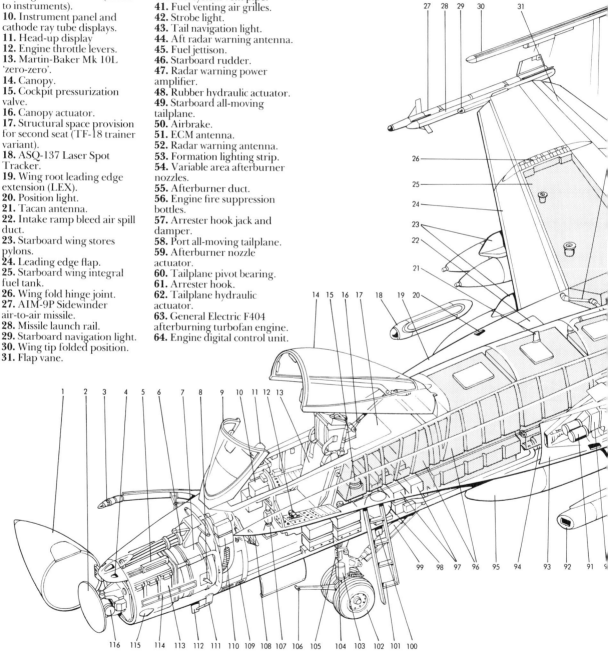

83. AIM-7 Sparrow air-to-air missile.
84. Mainwheel shock absorber strut.
85. Inboard stores pylon.
86. Main undercarriage pivot bearing.
87. Hydraulic retraction jack.
88. Radar equipment cooling air spill valves.
89. External fuel tank.
90. Air conditioning system heat exchanger.

91. Radar equipment liquid cooling units.
92. AAS-38 forward looking infra-red (Flir) pod.
93. Boundary layer splitter plate.
94. Air conditioning system water separator.
95. Centreline fuel tank.
96. Forward fuselage fuel tanks.
97. Avionics equipment bay.
98. Liquid oxygen converter.

99. Nose undercarriage hydraulic retraction jack.
100. UHF antenna.
101. Retractable boarding ladder.
102. Forward retracting nosewheels.
103. Nosewheel steering unit.
104. Landing/taxiing lamp.
105. Carrier approach lights.
106. Catapult strop link.
107. Control column.
108. Rudder pedals.

109. Gun gas vents.
110. Ammunition feed mechanism.
111. Pitot head.
112. UHF/IFF antenna.
113. Radar equipment module.
114. Formation lighting strip.
115. Forward radar warning antenna.
116. Radar scanner tracking mechanism.

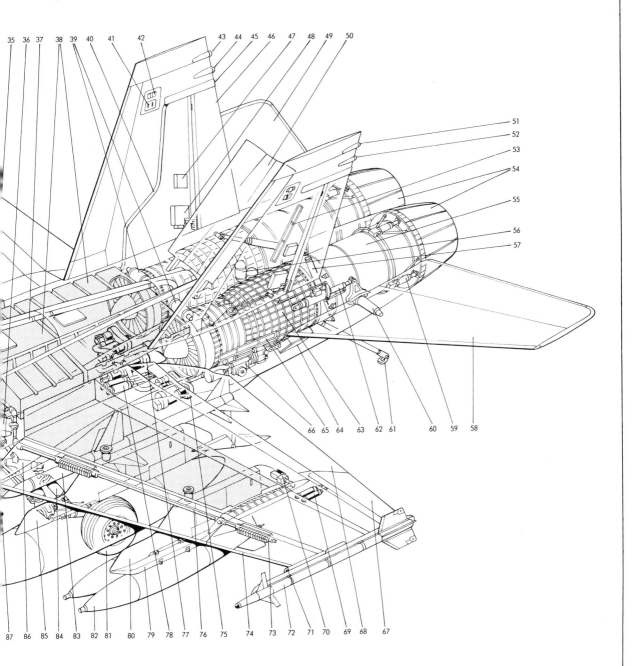

Above: Undercarriage and wheel well detail, leading edge extensions and AIM-7F Sparrow missile locations are clearly visible in this underside view of one of the nine FSD F-18A Hornets in landing configuration.

firewalls are fitted between the twin F404 engines. The fuselage is also employed for undercarriage stowage, the single-wheel main members retracting aft and rotating through 90 degrees so as to lie flat beneath the air intake ducts. The two-wheel nose gear retracts forward into a bay beneath the cockpit.

Another important aspect of the fuselage centres around the air intakes, which are fairly simple. Indeed, the only moving parts are two ducts—one to port and one to starboard—which permit bleed air to be ejected upwards into the flow field generated by the leading edge extension (LEX). The intake ramps/boundary layer splitter plates are fixed, being solid at the front end with perforations directly ahead of the inlet so as to permit sluggish boundary layer air to be disposed of via spill ducts in the upper fuselage.

The wing is vintage Northrop, having a trapezoidal planform and incorporating variable camber. Of cantilever construction with a six-spar machined aluminium alloy torsion box, the wing-fuselage attachment is by six dual-fork lugs, the wing being located in the mid-fuselage position with slight anhedral. Perhaps the most novel feature, though, is the LEX which protrudes forward to a point more or less adjacent to the front of the cockpit and which permits the F-18 to sustain controlled flight at very high angles of attack. This is not the only benefit for it greatly increases maximum lift while also reducing lift-induced and supersonic trim drag factors as well as limiting the intensity of buffet.

In fact, about the only disadvantage of LEX is that it is basically dead weight. Trim considerations make it unsuitable for the stowage of fuel, while it could not house gun armament without adding bulges which would disturb the airflow. However, the port LEX does serve as a neat and unobtrusive method of stowing the integral boarding ladder.

As far as control surfaces are concerned, the F-18's wing has few surprises. Variable camber is achieved by full-span leading edge flaps and hydraulically-actuated single-slotted trailing edge flaps. Not surprisingly, computers are used to manage extension and retraction, setting the most desirable angle to give optimum performance throughout the envelope. Hydraulically-driven ailerons can double as flaps to enhance low speed handling qualities, while differential operation of flaps and ailerons is used for roll control. With regard to materials, the primary trailing edge flaps employ graphite/epoxy composite skins, while all other wing-located control surfaces utilise aluminium skinning. Finally, the outer panel is hinged at the inboard end of each aileron for stowage.

The fully-variable horizontal tailplanes use aluminium honeycomb construction with graphite epoxy skinning, aluminium leading and trailing edges, and titanium reinforcement around the attachment points. Hydraulically actuated, they may be used in concert for pitch control or differentially for roll control, doubling as "tailerons" in the latter instance so as to augment aileron performance which, in certain circumstances, may be inadequate.

Turning to the vertical tail, the fins are of cantilever construction with graphite epoxy skinning and titanium leading edges. Small panels of the latter material are used to cover the hydraulic actuators of the rudders which are single-piece aluminium units with graphite epoxy skins.

A "flutter" problem

Six fin-to-fuselage attachment frames should have provided sufficient strength, but it was fatigue in this area which prompted a grounding order in late 1984 when it was discovered that turbulent air from the LEX was impinging on the tops of the fins and causing them to "flutter". Indeed, the severity of the lateral movement of the fins was such that it could be seen clearly with the naked eye and it didn't take long to discover fatigue-induced cracks on a number of aircraft. Incorporating a "fix" was a costly exercise, for a large number of Hornets had been completed

by this time and these all had to be rectified at McDonnell Douglas' expense. The modification involved "beefing up" the fin-to-fuselage attachment points.

Fly-by-wire controls

Looking beneath the skin, perhaps the most interesting feature is the quadruple digital fly-by-wire (FBW) control system, the first of its kind installed in a production aircraft. In simple terms, stick and rudder inputs are noted by a computer which issues the desired commands to the various control surfaces, while at the same time not allowing the pilot to overstress the airframe. In the best traditions of democracy, this system works by "majority vote". Thus, in the event of one system failing, the other three will override it. Indeed, FBW redundancy is such that, should a second system fail, as long as the two which remain are in agreement, control can still be exercised. In the unlikely event of total failure, direct electrical back-up exists for all control surfaces, while for worst-case situations the pilot can employ direct mechanical back-up to the horizontal tail

Below: Centre and aft fuselage sections complete with vertical tail surfaces are prepared for shipment by Northrop personnel at El Segundo, California. Upon arrival at St Louis, they will be mated with major sub-assemblies produced by the prime contractor, McDonnell Douglas.

surfaces, this providing some pitch and roll control.

Duplicate hydraulic systems are provided, these being routed separately as far as possible as a result of experience gained in South-East Asia when many F-105 Thunderchiefs were lost due to both of the virtually adjacent systems being rendered inoperative by a single shell.

Hornet powerplant

General Electric is responsible for Hornet propulsion, which is provided by twin F404-GE-400 low-bypass turbofans located side by side in the aft fuselage. Development of the F404 ran almost concurrently with that of the P-530 Cobra/YF-17/F-18 series. It originated as the GE 15 in the late 1960s and flew for the first time as the YJ101 in the YF-17 during June 1974. Like the basic airframe, the engine has "grown" significantly, evolution into the F404 being accompanied by an increase in thrust to the present afterburner-augmented rating of 16,000lb st (7258kg st).

In its present form as the F404-GE-400, the engine is broadly similar to the YJ101, although it is about 10 per cent bigger and has a slightly greater bypass ratio of 0.34. Modular construction permits entire sections to be changed quickly, while the relatively small size is a key factor in keeping weight down and has the added advantage of facilitating maintenance at sea. The entire unit is designed so that engineers

Above: Small is beautiful. Two examples of the General Electric's diminutive F404-GE-400 turbofan power the Hornet; modular construction greatly eases maintenance workloads. Each engine is 158in (403cm) long, 34.8in (88cm) in diameter, and weighs 2,000lb (907kg). Time from idle to full afterburning thrust is under seven seconds.

can drop it out of the belly of the aircraft.

In the normal course of events, routine engine servicing is made much simpler by the in-flight engine condition monitoring system (IECMS). This monitors performance electronically, notifying faults to the pilot and preparing a read-out for maintenance troops. Engine accessories are readily accessible through the engine bay doors, and the maintenance task is eased by the adoption of line replaceable units (LRUs).

Remarkably responsive engine

Although it is basically new and unproven, the F404 has encountered few serious difficulties; and one plus factor is an extreme resistance to compressor stall even at high angles of attack. Even on the rare occasions when a stall can be induced, this problem corrects itself very quickly with engine and afterburner relight occurring automatically. No less welcome is the fact that the engine has proved remarkably responsive, being able to accelerate from idle to full afterburner in less than four seconds. On the negative side, specific fuel consumption and the time taken to accelerate from Mach 0.8 to Mach 1.6 originally fell slightly short of desired levels. Correcive measures have gone some way towards making good these failings but they have not been entirely overcome.

Perhaps the most serious engine-related problem occurred on 8 September 1980 when Hornet T2 (Bu.No.160784) suffered an explosive failure of the low-pressure turbine disc on the starboard engine after appearing at the Farnborough Air Show. Despite a determined attempt to reach Boscombe Down, pilot Jack Krings was unable to manipulate the port engine throttle and, faced with an increasingly uncontrollable aircraft, he and his rear-seat passenger—Lieutenant Colonel Gary Post of the Marine Corps—eventually had to part company with the Hornet which crashed at Middle Wallop, Hampshire. Unfortunately, the ensuing investigation was hampered by loss of part of the disc and no firm cause was ever established, although the general opinion was that a manufacturing defect was probably responsible.

Auxiliary power unit

One aspect of the Hornet likely to be of great value when operating from austere airfields is the auxiliary power unit (APU), a 200-hp Garrett AiResearch device which removes the need for external power sources. Located in the aircraft's belly, the APU is started by the F-18's battery, and thereafter acts as a source of high-pressure air for the turbine starter.

Below: An F-18 accelerates skywards away from the McDonnell Douglas facility at Lambert Field, St. Louis. This photograph particularly emphasises the excellent all-round visibility enjoyed by F-18 pilots.

Above: The extremely narrow head-on profile of the Hornet makes it such a difficult adversary to "eyeball". This test aircraft was undergoing early sea trials. Note the folded wings, leading edge extensions, flaps and ailerons.

Once one engine is running, bleed air may be diverted to start the second F404.

Moving on to fuel, the F-18 has a total internal capacity of 11,000lbs (4,990kgs) of JP-4 or JP-5, contained in six self-sealing, foam-protected tanks. The entire fuel system is carefully designed to as to minimise the fire risk. A typical example of attention to detail is provided by the fact that the only fuel lines which enter the engine compartments are the main feeds to each engine fuel control. In this way, the risk of a severed fuel line discharging into the engine bay is reduced.

For long-range missions, internal fuel capacity may be augmented by up to three 350-US gallon (1,325-litre) external tanks. When operating in this con-figuration the F-18A has a maximum fuel load of around 17,800lbs (8,074kgs) while the two-seat TF-18A is able to accommodate about six per cent less internal fuel.

Refuelling is accomplished via a single point on the port side of the front fuselage. Naturally, the F-18 is also configured for in-flight refuelling. The probe is positioned just ahead of the cockpit on the starboard side of the nose section, while two fuel dump vents are located near the top of each vertical tail directly above the rudder.

3
Testing the Hornet

THE MAIDEN flight of the first FSD Hornet in November 1978 was, understandably, a high point in the programme, such an occasion always being a time of anxiety for those closely involved. For the Hornet, this hurdle was negotiated safely, albeit somewhat behind schedule. The first flight, of course, actually heralded the start of an intensive test and evaluation effort which eventually culminated in the Hornet being cleared for operational service with combat units of the US Navy and Marine Corps.

As far as the F-18 programme was concerned, those responsible for overseeing the test effort elected to adopt a single-site concept in which virtually all of the many test objectives were accomplished from just one base. In view of the splendid resources which existed there, the designated site was Naval Air Station (NAS) Patuxent River, Maryland, home of the Naval Air Test Centre (NATC) and long associated with research and development.

Accordingly, McDonnell Douglas personnel transferred to Patuxent River and set about the FSD programme in January 1979. They worked in close co-operation with their Navy colleagues for almost four years, a period which witnessed over 3,000 flights encompassing such diverse aspects as basic handling qualities, avionics, carrier suitability and qualification, weapons release and performance.

Most of the responsibility for shouldering the burden of this test work fell to the 11 FSD machines, although towards the end of the programme a limited number of pilot-production Hornets also made a significant contribution. By then, the main thrust of test work was more concerned with operational applications and the number of sites involved had diversified as the aircraft moved inexorably nearer to fleet service.

For instance, the Pacific Missile Test Center's excellent range facilities were brought into play for missile firing trials. These were largely accomplished by VX-4 at Point Mugu, California, this being the

Below: Dummy AIM-7F Sparrow radar-guided air-to-air missiles are carried by Hornet number one (Bu.No.160775) during the course of a test sortie from Patuxent River. The Navy titles visible on this side of the aircraft were matched by Marines inscriptions to starboard.

Navy's principal fighter-dedicated Operational Test and Evaluation Force (OTAEF). Another OTAEF unit—VX-5 at China Lake, California—was more concerned with exploring the Hornet's potential as an attack aircraft, a task which used the vast inland range areas of the Naval Weapons Center.

In addition to these two units, personnel of the NATC were by no means idle, accomplishing such notable objectives as carrier suitability testing, a process that began at Patuxent River in 1979 with Hornet number three. This aircraft successfully completed more than 70 catapult launches and 120 arrested landings or "traps" on the NATC's "concrete aircraft carrier".

Thereafter, at the end of October 1979, the Hornet went to sea for the first time, spending four days aboard the USS *America* (CV-66) for a series of trials which assessed launch and recovery performance as well as less spectacular but no less relevant matters such as deck handling qualities. At the end of what was later described as "the most successful sea trials in Naval aviation history", the third Hornet fouled up badly at Oceana when the undercarriage failed on landing because of exposure to greater than anticipated stress levels while at sea. Fortunately, the aircraft sustained only minor damage and was soon back in action after this unfortunate incident which revealed the need for modifications to the undercarriage.

Almost inevitably, experience gained during the course of test flying indicated certain areas of deficiency, and this period was one of design "tweaking" which ensured that the product which eventually reached operational units was safe and capable of doing the job or jobs demanded of it. One classic instance of structural refinement which arose from flight test work concerned the LEX or, to be more specific, the slots cut into this distinctive feature. Assessment of the airflow pattern revealed that these generated an unacceptably high amount of drag which in turn signally affected acceleration and range characteristics. The solution was simple, the slots being filled in on Hornet number eight. This action went some way towards improving the F-18's range although it still fell short of specification.

Flying surfaces changed

Another modification which was also adopted witnessed the elimination of the notches or "snags" in the wing and horizontal tailplane leading edges, which were deleted for very different reasons. The notch in the wing went as part of a complex modification aimed at enhancing roll rate, while that in the tailplane was sacrificed to reduce the nosewheel lift-off speed which, at 140 knots (259km/h), was way too high. Deletion of the tailplane notch was just one measure—another involved modification of flight control system software—which helped bring rotation speed down to the far more acceptable mark of 115 knots (213km/h).

Weapon testing formed a major part of the project and one which was highly successful, although the fact that the Hornet possessed multi-role potential probably helped to make it rather more complex than would normally be the case. Nevertheless, most of the objectives and obstacles seem to have been negotiated without too many problems. The test encompassed live firing trials of both missile and gun armament as well as examining stores release characteristics. Some of this work was performed by the FSD machines, while, as already noted, VX-4 and VX-5 also helped to explore the Hornet's offensive capability.

As far as clearing the various weapons for service

Below: FSD Hornet No.4 (Bu.No.160778) closes upon a drogue trailed by a Strategic Air Command KC-10A Extender during the course of in-flight refuelling trials.

se, missile firing tests began in December 1979 with the AIM-9 Sidewinder being employed for the first time by Hornet number five against a BQM-34 Firebee drone. Company pilot Bill Lowe was in command on this occasion and had he been engaging an enemy aircraft there can be no doubt that he would have emerged victorious for the missile actually passed within three feet (0.9m) of the target drone. This achievement was surpassed in later tests, Sparrow and Sidewinder weapons scoring no less than five direct hits in the first eight firings.

Testing the gun

Evaluation of the Vulcan M61A1 20mm cannon was also encouraging and confirmed that, despite its proximity to the APG-65 radar, it had little or no effect on this important piece of equipment or, for that matter, on engine operation. The cannon's position above the nose apparently limited the possibility of engine stalls induced by gas ingestion. Ground evaluation included emptying the 570-round magazine in a single sustained burst while aerial testing witnessed full discharge in six short bursts of fire.

Weapons testing also thoroughly explored ground

Below: Bombs and AIM-9 Sidewinder missiles adorn the weapons racks of the fourth F-18A, which was mainly engaged in structural flight test duties.

attack capability. One early lesson resulted in the decision to move the external racks forward by some five inches (127mm) so as to counteract a mild flutter problem. Various weapons and combinations of weapons were evaluated during the course of this programme, one notable highlight being a simulated attack mission mounted against the Pinecastle range in central Florida on 13 October 1981.

Operating from Patuxent River, the Hornet involved—a pilot production machine, (Bu.No 161248)—was loaded with four Mk.83 1,000lb (454kg) low-drag "slick" bombs, two AIM-9 Sidewinders and three 315-US gallon (1192 litre) auxiliary fuel tanks as well as laser spot tracker/strike camera (LST/SCAM) and Flir pods and a full magazine for the Vulcan cannon. Airborne for just over three hours, the F-18 accomplished this mission unrefuelled, performing a touch-and-go approach on its return to Patuxent River before recovering with about 1,200lbs (544kgs) of fuel remaining at shutdown. This was a quite adequate reserve when one considers that the distance to the range was some 620 miles (998 kms) and that production-configured Hornets carry an additional 700lbs (318kgs) of fuel.

As far as external stores are concerned, apart from relocation of the racks, the only other significant change concerned the auxiliary fuel tanks and even this worked to the F-18's advantage. Initially, it was decided to utilize tanks of elliptical cross-section so as

to provide a slightly greater margin of clearance. Unfortunately, testing of this design quickly revealed that it was ill-suited for the rigours of routine carrier-borne operations and it was therefore replaced by a tank of more conventional cylindrical form, which was able to accommodate an additional 15 US gallons (68 litres) of fuel.

A far less visible but no less demanding series of tests was accomplished under USAF auspices by the McKinley Climatic Laboratory at Eglin AFB, Florida. Conducted well away from prying eyes in the security of a large hangar, this programme subjected the Hornet to the extremes of climate that it is likely to experience during the course of its operational career. Once again, it appears to have passed the tests with flying colours despite being firmly grounded for this aspect of the development effort.

During the course of climatic assessment, the F-18 was subjected to extreme temperature—varying from −65 degrees F (−54 degrees C) to +125 degrees F (+52 degrees C)—as well as other meteorological phenomena including winds of up to 100mph (161km/h), "tropical rainstorms", with precipitation rates rising as high as 20ins (508mm) per hour, and "blizzards".

Almost inevitably, the testing period was marred by a couple of accidents, happily without fatalities being involved. The first casualty concerned TF-18A

Above: Carrier suitability trials were predominantly the preserve of the third FSD Hornet, Bu.No.160777, seen here moments before "trapping" aboard the USS *Dwight D. Eisenhower* in February 1982.

Bu.No.160784, which crashed in England following an engine explosion after appearing at the Farnborough Air Show in September 1980. This embarrassing loss was quickly attributed to engine failure. However, far more puzzling was the second crash, when pilot-production Hornet Bu.No.161215 met a watery grave in the Chesapeake Bay on 14 November 1980, less than a week before the first Hornet squadron commissioned at Lemoore.

On this occasion, Navy pilot Lt C. Brannon of VX-4 lost control while undertaking what should have been a routine handling sortie from nearby Patuxent River. Despite vigorous efforts to regain control, Brannon eventually had no option but to eject, although he was soon retrieved from the chilly waters of the Bay and was able to relate the circumstances surrounding this mysterious accident to the investigating team.

Even so, it took some weeks to recreate the loss of control, McDonnell Douglas and Navy test pilots logging well over 100 sorties with Hornet No.6 (Bu.No.160780) which was the original spin test aircraft. Fitted with an anti-spin recovery parachute between the tail surfaces, 160780 did eventually duplicate Brannon's departure from controlled flight. On this occasion the pilot managed to regain control by employing differential thrust settings on the two engines, one being brought back to flight idle and the other being advanced to full afterburner.

Basically, it appears that one of the computers had been the culprit, when its logic did not permit Brannon to exercise full control authority, presumably for fear of overstressing the structure. Rectification was simple, in that a spin-recovery switch was installed, which enabled a pilot to override the computer and employ whatever corrective measures he felt necessary. A further carefully-staged repetition of the circumstances surrounding the loss of control confirmed the efficacy of this "fix".

Special instrumentation

In the test aircraft, the cockpit displays were programmed to blank out when yaw rates exceeding 15 degrees per second were experienced, the system then providing visual indication of the direction in which the control column should be moved to accomplish recovery. Fitted to test aircraft and early production Hornets, this switch will eventually no longer be necessary, owing to improvements to the computerized system taking its place.

Since then, despite the fact that the number of flying hours logged annually has steadily increased as more and more aircraft have become available, the Hornet has demonstrated a remarkably consistent safety record; and only a handful have been lost following its entry into service (and one of those was a test specimen).

Below: The waters of the Chesapeake Bay are the backdrop for this view of the flight line at Patuxent River with the first two single-seaters awaiting their turn to fly.

Tragically, though, one of the most recent accidents known to have occurred claimed the life of Henry "Hank" Kleeman, the former boss of VF-41 "Black Aces", who, while flying an F-14A Tomcat played a major part in the destruction of two Libyan Sukhoi Su-22 "Fitters" over the Gulf of Sidra on 19 August 1981. Having in the meantime been promoted from the rank of Commander to Captain Kleeman died when the Hornet he was piloting overturned on landing at Miramar, California, on 3 December 1985.

By then, major obstacles on the path to operational service, such as Board of Inspection and Survey (BIS) trials, had been safely negotiated and the Hornet was well established with Navy and Marine Corps units. Examples of the type had been deployed aboard the aircraft carriers of both the Atlantic and Pacific Fleets during 1985.

Good progress overseas

Turning to overseas customers, despite some delay arising from problems with the vertical tail surfaces, Canada's CF-18 was in daily use in 1985 at air bases in Canada and West Germany. Australia's training programme was also making excellent progress towards activation of the first operational unit in the summer of 1986, coincidentally at about the same time as deliveries to Spain are scheduled to get under way. On balance, then, those most closely associated with the Hornet clearly have every reason to be well satisfied with what they have achieved so far.

Although it may look complicated, the Hornet cockpit is carefully laid out so as to ease pilot workload as much as possible. Consequently, it is dominated by three cathode ray tube displays which can be used to present a multitude of information relating to aircraft systems and the developing tactical situation. Using the HOTAS (hands on throttle and stick) concept, all switches needed in air-to-air and air-to-ground combat are located on the control column (seven switches) or throttle (ten switches).

1: Head-up display (HUD). 2: Master monitor display. 3: Canopy jettison lever. 4: Engine monitor display. 5: Launch bar/arrester hook bypass control and stores jettison selectors. 6: Fuel quantity indicator. 7: ECM panel. 8: Horizontal situation display. 9: Caution light panel. 10: Landing gear deployment controls. 11: Arrester hook controls. 12: Magnetic compass. 13: Radar warning receiver display. 14: Artificial horizon. 15: Multi-function display. 16: Up-front control panel.

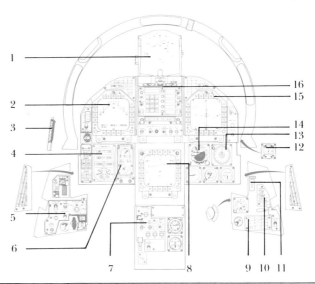

Above: No.410 Squadron's official crest features a Cougar, but is not normally displayed on actual aircraft of this unit.

Above: Unit insignia as applied by No.410 Squadron to its CF-18s consists of this stylized low visibility Cougar.

151-01

Above: Displaying the insignia of No.410 (Cougar) Squadron on the top of the vertical tail surfaces, CF-18B 188902 was the second example of the McDonnell Douglas/Northrop fighter delivered to the Canadian Armed Forces.

Above: Australian Hornets are represented here by an artist's rendition of the first single-seat F-18A (A21-1) which will be delivered to the RAAF during 1986.

Below: The first example of an *Ejercito del Aire* Hornet to make its debut was two-seat TF-18A CE.15-1 which was rolled out at St Louis in the latter half of 1985.

Above: Maintenance crew boot marks have made this Marine Hornet look dirty and mean during Sixth Fleet flight operations off CV-43 USS *Coral Sea*, January 1986.

Above: Typical Hornet nose marking detail can be clearly seen on the VFA-125 TF-18A in the foreground. Visible behind it is the F-18A that is profiled on these pages.

Above and below: Bearing the name of Captain James Partington—the boss of VFA-125 "Rough Raiders" at Lemoore—beneath the cockpit, F-18A 161250/NJ-500 was one of the first Hornets to be delivered to a Navy squadron, VFA-125 having been chosen to get operational training under way. A mixed bag of bombs, air-to-air missiles and auxiliary fuel tanks are carried in these two drawings which depict the aircraft shortly after it was handed over at Lemoore.

Above: The US Navy's first operational Hornet squadron was VFA-113 "Stingers" at Lemoore. A "low-viz" variation of the insignia shown here is displayed on VFA-113's F-18As.

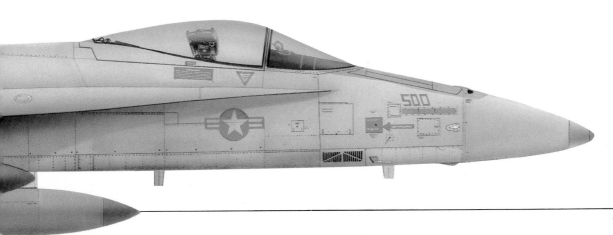

Above: One of four F-18A squadrons aboard *Coral Sea* recently, VMFA-314 was the first USMC unit to get the new fighter.

Above: VFA-131's squadron marking provides visible confirmation of the fact that it operates the F-18A Hornet.

Left: Typical upper surface F-18 markings are worn by this VFA-125 aircraft.

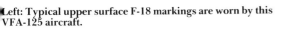

Above: CVW-13's "AK" code letter combination is displayed on the inner fin surfaces of VFA-132 Hornets.

Left: Sister squadron to VFA-131, the "Privateers" of VFA-132 also embarked on the *Coral Sea* for the 1985-86 deployment to the Mediterranean. The outer fin marking applied to Hornets of VFA-132 is depicted in this scrap view.

Below: VFA-131 "Wildcats" was the first operational Atlantic Fleet F-18 squadron.

Above: Much encumbered by a typical assortment of flight kit, a Hornet pilot surveys his high-tech instrument panel before setting out on a training mission.

Right: He sits on a Martin Baker Mk.SJU 5/6 ejection seat similar to the test specimen shown here. Possessing "zero-zero" capability, this is his last lifeline in the event of an emergency.

4
Avionics and Armament

LIKE MOST modern warplanes, the Hornet's angular appearance tends to blind the casual observer to what lies beneath the skin for it is here that much of the "magic" is worked, a highly sophisticated array of avionics being provided to assist the pilot in the execution of his mission. Although some of its opponents have argued that the work-load could exceed the capacity of one man, operating experience seems to indicate that this argument is unsound. But there is, of course, a wealth of difference between simulated combat training and the "real thing" and this is one of those questions which may never be answered.

The Hornet cockpit is designed to provide the pilot with as much information on the tactical situation as possible and in an easily digested form. Accordingly, less essential and less time-critical instruments are relegated to positions which, while by no means "out-of-sight", are "out-of-mind" for much of the time. In this way, the pilot can devote most of

his attention to the more urgent matters when in combat.

The F-18 is what is described as an integrated weapons systems, and it follows that the airframe is just one element of a complex package. In fact, it is probably fair to say that the Hornet represents a classic instance of the sum total being greater than that of the individual parts for virtually every aspect of the weapons system is interconnected. Also, a high degree of redundancy is built-in so as to avoid the risk of having to abort a mission in the event of the failure of a vital component.

There can be no doubt that the Hornet's radar is really the heart of the system, and virtually everything else is dependent upon it. Like everything else about the F-18, the original specification was most

Below: Ease of maintenance is one of the key features of the F-18's Hughes AN/APG-65 radar, technicians being able to gain access by simply swinging the radome aside and sliding the radar out. Line replaceable units permit rapid return to serviceable state in event of failure.

stringent, stipulating that the radar perform air-to-air, air-to-ground and navigation functions, be one-man operable, be small and easy to maintain, and be able to attain high levels of reliability. Westinghouse and Hughes felt confident that they could satisfy these requirements and duly submitted proposals, the Hughes contender being chosen in late 1977.

Given the service designation AN/APG-65, the Hughes radar is a coherent pulse-Doppler type operating in the X-band (8-12.5GHz). Since it is expected to operate in air-to-air and air-to-ground modes, the APG-65 is in many ways a compromise solution and one could therefore expect overall capability to be degraded as a result of the Navy's desire to have a "jack of all trades" in a single system. That this does not seem to have occurred says much for the Hughes Radar Systems Group.

Air-to-air radar modes

Taking the air-to-air mission first, the APG-65 can be employed in a variety of modes to meet a variety of situations. First, it is obviously desirable to detect targets at extreme range if only for the simple fact that the pilot can use this information to manoeuvre into an advantageous tactical position. The velocity search (VS) mode basically fulfils this function, permitting targets to be detected at ranges in excess of 80 nautical miles (148kms) and providing data on azimuth and velocity. It is prioritized to pay attention only to those returns which are closing on (approaching) the F-18.

Conversely, the range-while-search (RWS) mode

presents information on all contacts occupying that portion of sky ahead of the Hornet at ranges of between 40 and 80 nautical miles (74-148kms). At ranges of less than 40 nautical miles, the pilot can switch to the track-while-scan (TWS) mode in which the APG-65 is able to maintain ten target track files, displaying eight of these at any time. Additional data pertaining to the contact presenting the greatest threat is also displayed. This typically includes information on aspect, altitude and velocity.

Closely allied subsidiary modes include a single target track (STT) capability which is automatically designated on the HUD if a specific target should come within range when the radar is operating in the RWS mode. Information presented to the pilot via the HUD includes steering commands and weapon launch data, and the system also provides a "shoot" cue when and if a firing solution is attained.

Another valuable feature of the APG-65 is the raid assessment mode in which the beam may be "sharpened" so as to examine more closely the area around a specific return and ascertain whether this emanates from a single target or if it relates to a group of aircraft in fairly close formation.

Moving on to actual air combat, there are three

Below: The Hornet's AN/APG-65 radar offers a variety of air-to-ground modes to aid the pilot. Left: Air-to-surface ranging mode provides data on target distance.

Centre: Fixed and moving ground target track modes employ two-channel monopulse angle tracking to locate precisely a target.

Right: Sea surface search mode utilises "filtering" of radar returns to permit targets such as capital ships to be detected and attacked.

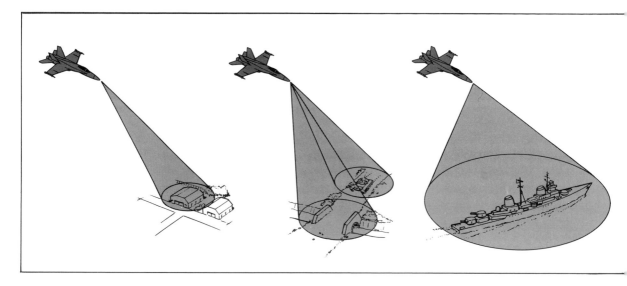

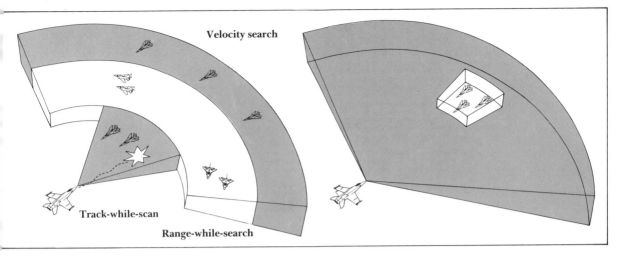

Velocity search

Track-while-scan

Range-while-search

Above: The multi-mode capability of the AN/APG-65 radar enables it to perform velocity search (for long-range detection), range-while-search (to detect anything up to 80nm/150km distance) and track-while scan functions (for closing phases of engagements).

Above: In the raid assessment mode, Doppler beam sharpening permits AN/APG-65 to examine one return and see if it relates to several aircraft in close formation. This mode is effective at up to 30nm (55km) provided the enemy are at least 500ft (150m) apart, useful for closing phases.

KFT   TRKN
15797

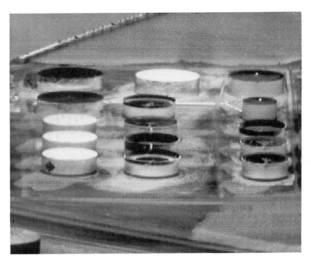

Above: Flir imagery from the AN/AAS-38 system provides a remarkably clear picture and is especially valuable in determining target location in poor weather or haze, as can be seen from these two photographs. That at left shows a surface vessel at sea, while that at right is of a POL storage facility.

Below: The AN/APG-65 in aerial combat: left, HUD acquisition mode; centre, vertical acquisition mode, valuable in a turning engagement; right, boresight mode, using a scan pattern aligned along aircraft centreline, most advantageous in 'tail-chase' encounters.

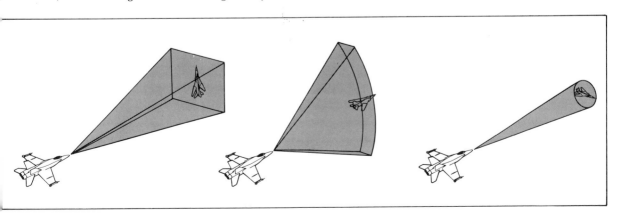

basic radar modes, each with its own particular advantages and disadvantages. The boresight mode is most likely to be used in the traditional "tail chase" type of engagement, and employs a very narrow 3.3 degree beam scanning only a small area of sky directly ahead of the aircraft. The vertical acquisition mode is perhaps of greatest value in an encounter when both target and tracker are turning hard, the radar scanning an arc 5.3 degrees wide and encompassing that portion of sky extending from 60 degrees above boresight axis (centreline) to 14 degrees below. In this mode, all the pilot theoretically has to do to achieve automatic lock-on is to roll his aircraft into the same plane of motion as that of the target, ideally positioning it just above the canopy bow and aligned vertically with the HUD. The third mode is head-up display acquisition in which the antenna

scans a "box" corresponding to the field of view of the HUD itself. This box extends to 10 degrees left and right of the centreline, 14 degrees above and 6 degrees below.

In all of these modes—which are effective at ranges varying from 500 feet (152m) to five nautical miles (9kms)—the radar automatically locks-on to the first target acquired. Visual confirmation is given on the cockpit CRT displays, the HUD and by flashing lights located on the canopy bow. However, the pilot may override the system, as a "walk-through" facility permits him to reject successive targets until he acquires that most desired. Alternatively, he can employ a moveable cursor for target designation.

Gun direction mode

The last air combat-orientated facility is the gun director mode—employed at ranges of less than five nautical miles (9kms)—in which the radar provides data pertaining to target position, range and velocity to drive the gun-aiming point on the HUD, this being the traditional "pipper". All the pilot then has to do is position the "pipper" on his selected target and squeeze the trigger, an act which is rather less simple than it sounds.

Although perhaps possessing a rather less extensive range of applications, the APG-65's air-to-ground capability is no less valuable. The primary real beam ground mapping mode is most useful for identifying substantial geographical features at long range so as to permit fairly precise landfall when, for instance, approaching enemy territory from the sea. Presentation takes the form of a small-scale radar map of the terrain which lies ahead. The data displayed is computer-corrected so as to provide a vertical image, rather than the oblique one which the radar itself sees.

Subsidiary mapping modes also employ Doppler beam "sharpening" so as to provide better resolution for navigation and target location, there being two such facilities available. In the first "sector" mode, a ratio of 19:1 is employed, which facilitates the recognition of significant topographical features. In this way, accuracy of *en route* navigation may be confirmed while it also permits specific locations—such as the initial point (IP) at which the attack phase of a mission actually begins—to be precisely identified. In he "patch" mode, normally employed during the terminal phases of weapons delivery, the ratio is 67:1 which enables the target to be identified at the earliest possible moment.

Although the Hornet lacks automatic terrain-following capability, the radar can be employed for terrain avoidance. Basically, this mode informs the pilot where the ground is in relation to his aircraft, leaving the finer detail of avoiding flying into it to his judgement. It can be pre-set to the required altitude, and the display then presents a visual reference to any obstacles which exceed the specified level so that the pilot can initiate avoiding action.

In addition to these air-to-ground modes, the Hughes radar is also employed for ranging and attack functions and can deal with fixed or moving targets. Automatic acquisition of a designated target is a feature of the system which may also be employed to provide ranging information when target designation is accomplished by either a laser spot

tracker/strike camera (LST/SCAM) or by forward-looking infra-red (Flir).

Last, but by no means least, the APG-65 also possesses a sea surface search mode. When used in this way, the radar's first action is to check sea state and, with the aid of computer analysis, establish the degree of "clutter". Having ascertained this, "filtering" of the ensuing returns leaves only those which are likely to indicate ships.

Excellent reliability

As can be seen, the Hornet radar is an impressive piece of equipment but perhaps even more remarkable is the level of reliability, which surpassed the specified 106-hour mean time between failure (MTBF) level rather earlier than allowed for by the schedule. When failures do occur, these are almost invariably identified and isolated by built-in test equipment (BITE). All that is then necessary is for the offending weapon replaceable assembly (WRA) to be "pulled" and substituted by a serviceable unit, a process which takes no more than 12 minutes.

Below: Graphically illustrating the multiplicity of ordnance which can be carried by Hornet, this picture shows the third aircraft with a typical assortment of weapons.

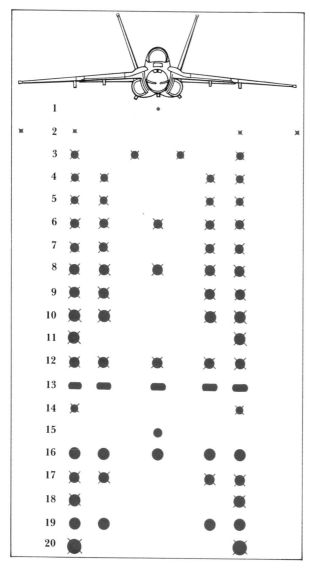

Above: Possible weapons combinations which may be carried by the F–18A Hornet are depicted here. 1: Vulcan M61 20mm cannon with 570 rounds of ammunition. 2: AIM-9 Sidewinder. 3: AIM-7F Sparrow. 4: AGM-65E Maverick. 5: AGM-88A HARM (High-speed Anti-Radiation Missile). 6: Mk82 LD/HD bomb. 7: Mk82 LGB. 8: Mk83 LD bomb. 9: Mk83 LGB. 10: Mk84 LD bomb. 11: Mk84 LGB. 12: Mk20 or CBU-59/B Rockeye. 13: BLU-95 FAE II. 14: AGM-62 Walleye. 15: Walleye data link pod. 16: Mk76/106 practice bomb dispenser. 17: BDU-12/20. 18: BDU-36. 19: LAU-10D/A, -61A/A or -68B/A launchers. 20: B-57 or B-61 nuclear bomb. Up to three auxiliary fuel tanks may also be carried.

The defective WRA is then examined by the USM-469 Radar Test System (RTS) which can provide visual and printed confirmation of where the fault lies. It is then usually a relatively simple task to restore the failed component to serviceable condition. Following repair, the WRA is again examined by RTS to check that it is functioning correctly before going back "on-the-shelf". With such a sophisticated "trouble-shooting" device, it is vital that the USM-469 RTS operates satisfactorily.

Data processing capability is an integral part of the modern warplane and the Hornet is not lacking in this area, possessing some two dozen computers with a combined memory exceeding that of the F-15 Eagle. Broadly speaking, the computers fall into two categories, namely sensor-related and mission-related. Those in the former are mainly concerned with functions of a detection and navigation nature while the latter are preoccupied with weapons delivery and display management, but each category is able to call upon the services of its own Control Data Corporation AN/AYK-14 64K core memory capacity computer.

Virtually none of the data generated by on-board sensors is likely to be of much use to the pilot in its raw form, and the computers make a significant contribution by converting it into a readily comprehensible format upon which he may base his actions. At the same time, they also alleviate work-load by performing countless calculations far more rapidly and accurately than the human brain. Thus, for example, the extremely complex equations—encompassing such criteria as ballistics, windage, velocity and altitude—which relate to accurate weapons delivery are accomplished by computer, release cues being notified by means of the HUD and other displays.

Advanced cockpit layout

Much comment has already been made of the cockpit layout, some pilots apparently drawing a parallel between it and *Star Wars*. Although perhaps overstating the case, there is no doubt that it is much more advanced than that of comparable fighters, making extensive use of digital and CRT displays, computer-generated symbology and push-button controls. However, the enthusiasm with which these features have been greeted has perhaps tended to overshadow the fact that a pilot still has to have sufficient skill to manoeuvre his aircraft into that point in space from which a successful kill or an accurate bombing pass may be made. Modern technology can make his job easier but, like all computer-based systems, it has to be vulnerable to the "GIGO" (garbage in, garbage out) syndrome. Instances have been already seen—admittedly on civilian aircraft—

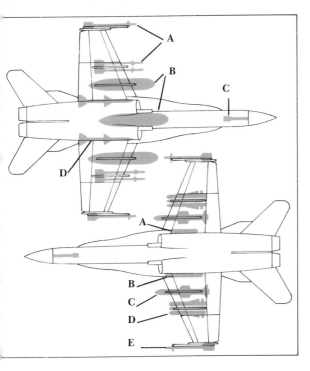

Above: Typical weapons combinations are depicted in these two drawings. In the air-to-air role, seen at the top, stores displayed are: A, AIM-9 Sidewinder; B, auxiliary fuel tanks; C, Vulcan M61 20mm cannon; D, AIM-120 AMRAAM or AIM-7F Sparrow. In air-to-ground or anti-shipping configuration, the F-18 may carry: A, AN/AAS-38 Flir pod; B, AN/ASQ-137 laser spot tracker; C, AGM-109 Harpoon; D, AGM-65 Maverick; E, AIM-9 Sidewinder.

where computer-based cockpit displays have gone blank; fortunately without dire consequences for those on board at the time.

As well as the computers, the Hornet's electronic wizardry includes Itek's AN/ALR-67 radar warning receiver (RWR) set, a pretty smart piece of equipment which has the ability to detect, isolate, classify and initiate countermeasures against a variety of electronic "threats". Visual reference as to the whereabouts of the threat is conveyed to the pilot by means of a cockpit display and he can also elect to take more overt countermeasures, using chaff and flares to further confuse enemy defences.

For the strike role, the F-18 can carry two special pods on those external stores stations which would more normally be used by AIM-7 Sparrow missiles. The devices concerned are Ford Aerospace's AN/AAS-38 forward-looking infra-red (Flir) pod and Martin-Marietta's AN/ASQ-173 laser spot tracker/strike camera (LST/SCAM) package, these being mounted to port and starboard respectively. The Flir unit is mainly intended to enhance all-weather/night

attack capability. Data from this device is presented in televisual form on one of the cockpit CRTs, while the fact that it is fully integrated with other avionics enables information to be used in the calculation of weapons release solutions. The LST/SCAM also permits accurate bombing in poor weather or bad visibility although it achieves this objective differently, with the tracking device locking-on to laser energy reflected by a pre-designated target and providing information on target location to cockpit displays and mission computers for weapon aiming and release.

The Hornet's sting

As far as weaponry is concerned, Hornet capability is impressive and the aircraft is compatible with a vast array of ordnance, encompassing air-to-air missiles, air-to-surface missiles, conventional "iron" bombs and "smart" weapons.

The primary weapons, when employed in the air-to-air role, are the AIM-7 Sparrow and the AIM-9 Sidewinder. Missile configurations may vary, the F-18 being able to operate with a maximum of six AIM-9s and two AIM-7s or, alternatively, four AIM-7s and two AIM-9s. The Hornet is particularly well-equipped for target detection, and if it can be said to have an "Achilles heel" in aerial combat, this probably relates to the Sparrow missile. Although a well-proven weapon, Sparrow does require the target to be constantly illuminated by the aircraft's own radar in order that it can home on reflected radar energy. Thus, at present, the F-18 can only engage

Below: Displaying the Aerospace Engineering Test Establishment's distinctive dayglo "X" marking on the fin, the first Canadian Armed Forces CF-18B (188901) delivers a batch of eight BL755 cluster bomb units during the course of weapons testing from Cold Lake, Alberta. Cameras mounted beneath the fuselage and wing tips recorded the drop for subsequent analysis by AETE.

one target at a time with this weapon. This has to make it vulnerable to a well-executed counter-attack. Looking to the future, however, the advent of the fire-and-forget AIM-120 AMRAAM will give multi-target potential while also limiting the risk of the F-18 being destroyed by another enemy fighter.

The third weapon which may be employed in aerial combat is the Vulcan M61A1 20-mm cannon which also has air-to-ground applications. Total ammunition capacity is 570 rounds, with a maximum rate of fire around 100 rounds per second. Perhaps the biggest apparent drawback of this weapon is its position ahead of the pilot. Nevertheless, night firing trials seem to indicate that muzzle flash is not a problem or, at least, not a serious one.

Air-to-ground payload

In air-to-ground mode, the weapons options are truly bewildering, especially if target detection devices are fitted. With regard to payload potential, the F-18A may operate with up to 17,000lbs (7,711kgs) of ordnance, which typically includes a pair of wing-tip mounted AIM-9 Sidewinders for self-defence.

Such a payload would however rarely be carried and in more normal situations, auxiliary fuel tanks would almost certainly be fitted, the centreline and inner wing stations being able to pump in fuel. Offensive weaponry is then restricted to the two outer underwing hardpoints but the F-18 could still do a fair bit of damage, typical weapon configurations including four Mk.83 1,000lb (454kg) bombs or two Mk.84 2,000lb (907kg) bombs or four "Rockeye" cluster bomb units (CBUs) or, for a real heavyweight punch, two B57 or B61 tactical nuclear weapons.

As far as conventional ordnance is concerned, low-drag "slicks" and high-drag Snakeye retarded bombs may be employed while laser-guided Paveway versions of the Mk.82, Mk.83 and Mk.84 can be used

against pin-point targets. Other "smart" weapons with which the F-18 is compatible include electro optically guided devices such as the AGM-62 Walleye glide bomb and the AGM-65 Maverick air-to-surface missile. Both of these weapons feature a small television camera in the nose, which generates pictures which are presented on one of the cockpit displays. All the pilot then has to do is locate the target and lock on to it, as steering instructions are relayed automatically by data link. Later versions of Maverick incorporate imaging infra-red or laser seekers, which are particularly effective at night or in conditions of poor visibility.

Possessing greater range, the AGM-84 Harpoon is primarily intended for use against shipping and utilizes active radar homing during the terminal stages of flight. A "fire and forget" weapon, Harpoon is highly resistant to countermeasures, although perhaps its greatest disadvantage is that its radar cannot discriminate between "high" and "low" value targets. However, it is known that an imaging infra-red version is under consideration and this would appear to possess much greater potential.

In the future, the F-18 could also be employed as a "Wild Weasel" engaging enemy surface-to-air missile sites. Utilizing the AGM-88A high speed anti-radiation missile (HARM), the Hornet would accompany conventional strike aircraft, dealing with radar "threats" when necessary. Basically, the AGM-88A works in conjunction with the F-18's radar warning receiver and computers to detect, assess and determine which emitter presents the most serious threat. Having established that, missile launch follows, with the weapon homing automatically to the point of origin of the emissions as long as the designated radar continues to operate.

Below: An AIM-9 Sidewinder accelerates away from an F-18A of Marine Corps fighter-attack squadron VMFA-314 during a live-firing exercise held off the coast of California.

5

Hornet in Service

QUITE A FEW follow-on test and evaluation objectives had still to be satisfactorily negotiated when the first Hornets began to join the fleet and there was still much to be done before the F-18 could go to sea as a fully-operational and mission-ready fighting machine. Nevertheless, formal establishment of the first of three Fleet Replacement Squadrons (FRSs) on 13 November 1980 was a harbinger of the end of the development phase.

As had occurred with the F-14 Tomcat, a Pacific Fleet facilitity was selected to be the home for the first Hornet FRS, VFA-125 "Rough Raiders" being the unit concerned and Naval Air Station (NAS) Lemoore, California, the base. Located 40 miles (64kms) south of Fresno in the San Joaquin Valley, Lemoore is one of the most modern Naval Air Stations and in view of the fact that the Hornet is mainly viewed by the Navy as an A-7E Corsair replacement it was a logical choice for the F-18. At the time of VFA-125's creation, no fewer than ten deployable A-7E Corsair-equipped units were

assigned to this California base. Other elements of the Light Attack Wing Pacific (LAtWingPac) comprised an FRS with TA-7C and A-7E Corsairs and a Fleet Adversary Squadron with TA-4J Skyhawks.

Even the choice of VFA-125 was appropriate, for this squadron had previously served as a Corsair FRS at Lemoore until decommissioned in October 1977. At the time of its rebirth, production-configured F-18s had still to appear and it was therefore necessary to "borrow" a development aircraft, the machine chosen being Bu.No.161216 of the Naval Air Test Center.

Decked-out in a dark green fin top and rudder stripes, Bu.No.161216 looked very smart and may well have inspired Navy markings enthusiasts to hope that the era of low-visibility colours was nearing its end. Unfortunately, this colour scheme was by no means representative of that which would eventually

Below: The first Navy squadron to receive Hornets was VFA-125 at Lemoore, three "Rough Raiders" TF-18As sharing the flight line with a VX-4 F-18A in the spring of 1981.

find favour, but it is doubtful if such considerations bothered most of those present at the time.

In the event, VFA-125 had to wait until 19 February 1981 before receiving its first Hornet, this and the next two to arrive being redundant test specimens. Indeed, it was not until September 1981 that production F-18As and TF-18As began to reach the "Rough Raiders", but by year-end the number of aircraft on charge had risen to nine, and training of instructors and preparation of the syllabus had begun in earnest. However, occasional opportunities to explore the Hornet's capabilities did arise. One noteworthy test occurred in August 1981 when air combat manoeuvring (ACM) was conducted against a TA-4J Skyhawk of VA-127 and an F-5E Tiger II of the Fighter Weapons School.

Close-encounter training

This spell of ACM, accomplished over a four-day period, seems to have been very much a case of "feeling one's way", all engagements being "one-on-one". A far more ambitious ACM training period followed in January 1982 when VFA-125 despatched nine F-18s to Yuma, Arizona, in order to use the nearby air combat range for a series of "close encounters" with such types as the TA-4J, CF-5 and F-14A.

The deployment lasted three weeks and was mainly intended to firm up VFA-125's ACM syllabus, but it also enabled the squadron to complete ACM training against a mix of opponents in a variety of scenarios. Although "combat" with the Tomcat was confined to "one-on-one", engagements with other opponents more closely approximated to the real thing, odds against the F-18s sometimes rising as high as three to one.

In such engagements, it is naturally desirable to "kill" an "enemy" quickly and before he can begin to seek a position of advantage. Accordingly, these "battles" often opened with simulated Sparrow missile firings, subsequently degenerating into head-to-head situations in which those involved endeavoured to secure the upper hand and manoeuvre into a winning position. The Hornet's agility often gave VFA-125 pilots the edge.

Combat with the Tomcat was probably a different story, for Grumman's aircraft could use the long-range AIM-54 Phoenix to take out an opponent long before battle was joined. In a "dog-fight" situation, however, the two types would appear to be closely matched, pilot ability then becoming perhaps the most influential factor.

Maintenance and readiness

Deployments such as this naturally represented high points in the process of preparing to train personnel, but it should not be forgotten that much of the work, while being of a far less visible nature, was no less important. For instance, those who would ultimately maintain Hornet also had to acquire the necessary expertise. VFA-125's Fleet Readiness Aviation Maintenance Personnel (FRAMP) Department was to be responsible for providing specialized tuition to enlisted personnel.

By the summer of 1982, VFA-125's training programme had firmed up and personnel from the first operational unit began to arrive. The squadron chosen was a Marine Corps unit from El Toro, California, and the "Black Knights" of VMFA-314 duly began the process of transition on schedule at the beginning of August 1982. At this time, the "Rough Raiders" had still to undergo their first period of carrier qualification (carqual) operations.

Training with simulators

Despite the fact that this aspect of the training programme was not evaluated until September/October, "Black Knights" personnel were kept busy during the early stages of the five-month course. Initial instruction takes places in the Hornet Learning Center, where pilots attend lectures on the aircraft as well as employing audio-visual equipment to familiarize themselves with the new type. This phase of tuition is followed by time spent on the simulators which constitute an important part of VFA-125's training equipment and which enable a pilot to master many of the F-18's unique characteristics before he ever sets foot in the aircraft.

Simulator training begins in the part-task trainer (PTT) which is, essentially, a simplified Hornet cockpit. Here, the pilot is introduced to the hands on throttle and stick (HOTAS) philosophy, and spends some time acquiring the necessary skills to operate the various controls quickly and effectively. Then comes a sterner test in the shape of the operational

flight trainer (OFT), which simulates flight from take-off to touch-down, the visual displays being able to reproduce operations from either an airfield or an aircraft carrier.

The last simulator—and, undoubtedly, the most realistic—is the weapons tactics trainer (WTT), which comprises two 40ft (12m) domes with a cockpit in each and seven televisual projectors. As its title implies, the WTT is intended to provide the novice pilot with those skills which will enable him to get-the most out of his aircraft. Spending about 50 hours in the WTT, a student will receive advanced air-to-air radar training and some tuition in ACM tactics. It is possible to operate the domes either individually or as a pair to permit pilots in each dome to engage each other in "battle". Only after negotiating this hurdle satisfactorily does a pilot move on to actually flying the F-18 and even then he may well return to the WTT to "brush up" on particular aspects of the syllabus.

Flight training consists of around 70 sorties encompassing and expanding on those areas already examined in the simulators. Navy squadrons also complete 20 more sorties for "carqual" purposes while Marine Corps units don't appear necessarily to "carqual" although they almost certainly do undergo field carrier landing practice (FCLP) training. Thus, VMFA-314 did not go to sea for the first time until July 1983, some months after it had become operational. Then, it embarked aboard the USS Constella-

Above: Claiming the distinction of being the first fully-operational Hornet Squadron, VMFA-314 is normally resident at MCAS E1 Toro, California. One of its 12 aircraft is seen here during the course of in-flight refuelling from a Marine Corps KC-130 Hercules tanker.

tion (CV-64) for its first taste of life at sea, before eventually deploying aboard the USS Coral Sea (CV-43) in 1985.

That all lay in the future when, on 7 January 1983, VMFA-314 was declared operational at El Toro. At that time, it had only received five aircraft but the excellent serviceability meant that it was achieving rather more with this modest number than it had done with a full complement of F-4Ns.

Even as VMFA-314 was building up to full strength, the "Death Rattlers" of VMFA-323 were hard at work in transition. This unit duly began to receive the F-18 in early 1983, being completely equipped in June at about the same time as VMFA-314. So, by early summer of that year, the USMC's 3rd Marine Air Wing had two operational F-18 squadrons at El Toro with a third—the "Gray Ghosts" of VMFA-531—well advanced in transition.

Navy's first squadron

The focus of attention then switched to the Navy, and VA-113—most appropriately nicknamed the "Stingers"—was selected to be the first operational unit to convert from the A-7E to the Hornet. Formally redesignated VFA-113 on 25 March 1983, the

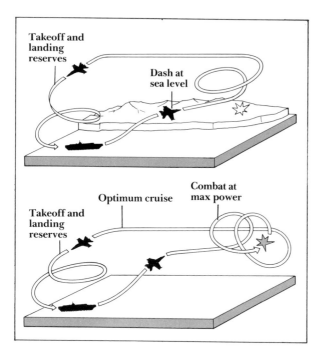

Above: Typical mission profiles are portrayed above. At the top, the lo-lo-hi strike profile involves an aircraft carrying three auxiliary fuel tanks, LST/SCAM and Flir pods, two AIM-9L Sidewinders and four Mk.83 GP bombs. In the interception mission, seen above, the standard weapon fit would comprise two AIM-7F Sparrows and two AIM-9L Sidewinders, plus the Vulcan M61 20mm cannon.

"Stingers" began transition a few days later, on 1 April, and eventually took delivery of the first of 12 aircraft on 16 August, two months ahead of schedule.

Fully occupied with transition between April and late-November, the "Stingers" returned to sea aboard the USS *Kitty Hawk* (CV-63) in mid-October, racking up the impressive tally of 260 arrested landings as they successfully accomplished day and night "carqual" objectives. After that, training continued until 25 November when VFA-125's FRS syllabus was completed.

The ensuing respite proved brief, VFA-113 going "on the road" when it deployed to Yuma on 27 November for three weeks of weapons and tactics training. This proved an outstanding success, as the F-18A's remarkable reliability permitted VFA-113 line crews to generate 30 per cent more sorties than planned. Taking ten aircraft to Yuma, the "Stingers" completed 403 sorties and logged some 427 flight hours. During this period they dropped over 900 Mk.76 25lb (11kg) practice bombs, 100 Mk.82 500lb (227kg) bombs and some Mk.83 1,000-pounders (454kg) as well as expending close to 4,000 rounds of

20mm ammunition during the air-to-ground phase. Attention then shifted to air-to-air, VFA-113's Hornets being pitted against oponents such as the F-5E, TA-4J, A-4F, F-4S and CF-5A, and once again the F-18 performed creditably.

Even as VFA-113's transition training programme was winding up, this unit's sister squadron—VFA-25 "Fist of the Fleet"—took delivery of its first Hornet on 11 November, an event that marked a high point in their conversion programme which had begun on 1 July 1983. Regaining operational status in early 1984, VFA-25 teamed up with VFA-113 as part of Carrier Air Wing 14 (CVW-14), the two squadrons working together as they prepared to make the Hornet's maiden operational deployment aboard the USS *Constellation* (CV-64). This cruise began on 21 February 1985, and entailed a visit to the Western Pacific and the Indian Ocean. The two squadrons spent approximately six months at sea in an extremely arduous tour which was, by all accounts, remarkably successful.

Lemoore retained sole responsibility for the Hornet transition programme throughout the remainder of 1983 and for virtually all of 1984 although the latter year was notable in that it witnessed establishment of the Atlantic Fleet's F-18 FRS (VFA-106 "Gladiators") at NAS Cecil Field, Florida, on 27 April. By then, however, VFA-125 had been instrumental in bringing three more squadrons into the expanding Hornet community.

"Wildcats" and "Privateers"

Destined to join Carrier Air Wing 13 (CVW-13), VFA-131 "Wildcats" was formally established at Lemoore on 3 October 1983 and was fairly well advanced with training when VFA-132 "Privateers" made its debut on 9 January 1984. These two units remained at Lemoore until 1 February 1985 when they transferred east to Cecil Field, in the process becoming the Atlantic Fleet's first two operational Hornet squadrons. Work-up trials and pre-deployment exercises aboard the USS *Coral Sea* (CV-43) kept them busy for much of 1985 and culminated in an operational readiness inspection which cleared the way for the Hornet's introduction to the Mediterranean. Interestingly, when the USS *Coral Sea* sailed from the US East Coast on 2 October 1985, it had no fewer than four F-18 squadrons aboard, VMFA-314 and VMFA-323 of the USMC

Above: With regard to US Navy Strike Fighter Squadrons, VFA-25 and VFA-113 were the first to deploy operationally with the Hornet, embarking aboard USS *Constellation* for a Western Pacific cruise in 1985. Here, aircraft from each squadron prepare to launch from "Connie".

occupying the slots that will eventually be taken by VFA-133 and VFA-134.

As far as the "Golden Hawks" were concerned, redesignation from VA-303 to VFA-303 on 1 January 1984 confirmed that the Naval Air Reserve Force is no longer regarded as a repository for obsolete aircraft types. Since it is manned by reservists who, naturally, have other commitments, the transition has been particularly lengthy. Indeed, clear evidence of just how lengthy is provided by the fact that VFA-303 was not expected to take delivery of its first Hornet until October 1985 while it is unlikely to have a full complement until well into 1986.

On a more general front, probably the most significant event of 1984 was the establishment of VFA-106 at NAS Cecil Field. The Atlantic Fleet's Hornet FRS, it has thus far kept a fairly low profile but it seems reasonable to assume that 1985 witnessed the start of training, one early candidate being VMFA-115 "Silver Eagles" from MCAS Beaufort which had begun to receive brand-new Hornets by September. Other new F-18s have also now been assigned to VFA-136 "Knight Hawks" and VFA-137 "Kestrels" which respectively formed at Lemoore and Cecil Field in July 1985.

Over on the West Coast, VFA-125 has been by no means idle, VFA-192 "Golden Dragons" and VFA-195 "Dambusters" being the newest Pacific Fleet squadrons to undergo transition, while April 1986 marked the beginning of Carrier Air Wing Five's transition, this com-

mand's four light attack and fighter units (VA-56, VA-93, VF-151 and VF-161) all being due to get the F-18 in time.

What is clear is that the Navy will eventually have no fewer than 42 Hornet squadrons, including six Reserve and two training units. As far as the Marines are concerned, they currently envisage a total of 12 front-line squadrons and an FRS and it is logical to expect Marine Reserve fighter-attack squadrons to also receive F-18s.

With the reconnaissance-dedicated RF-18 also due to enter the Navy inventory, the number of squadrons may well surpass the 60 mark although this would of course depend on the method of deployment adopted. However, since 100-120 RF-18s are required, the Navy may well organize a couple of dedicated reconnaissance units, assigning one to each major fleet. If this occurs, logical candidates would appear to be VFP-62 and VFP-63, both of which have performed this mission with distinction in the past.

In February 1986, it was announced that the Navy's prestigious "Blue Angels" aerobatic team will re-equip with 11 Hornets at the end of the 1986 display season.

As far as overseas air arms are concerned, only

Canada, Australia and Spain have selected the F-18 to date. Canada was the first when it revealed plans to purchase 137 examples in April 1980, this total being made up of 113 CF-18A single-seaters and 24 CF-18B two-seaters. For a time, it appeared that the number to be procured might be cut to 129 but a US Government decision to waive partially non-recurring development costs worked to Canada's advantage, permitting it to add an extra CF-18B as the 138th aircraft.

Intended to replace the CF-101 Voodoo, the CF-104 Starfighter and the CF-5A Freedom Fighter, production of Canada's CF-18s is being undertaken at St Louis, Missouri, and it was here that the first example (CF-18B 188901) made its debut on 28 July 1982.

Subsequently, on 25 October 1982, this and the second two-seater (188902) were delivered to the Aerospace Engineering Test Establishment (AETE) at Cold Lake, Alberta, an event predated by the creation of No.410 Fighter (Operational Training) Squadron at the same base in June 1982. Personnel assigned to No.410 "Cougar" Squadron had trained with VFA-125 and were in good shape when the first CF-18s reached Canada. Indeed, it was only five days later that No.410 Squadron took delivery of its initial aircraft and during the first two years of operation the programme proceeded satisfactorily, with the first operational squadron completing re-equipment more or less on time.

This was No.409 Squadron at Cold Lake, one of several CAF units engaged in the air defence mission, and it was followed by No.425 Squadron. Unfortunately for No.425, in Autumn 1984 problems with the vertical tail became apparent. This discovery led to the imposition of a grounding order or strict flying limitations across the entire fleet of

CF-18s. Naturally, this had significant impact on Canadian re-equipment, No.425 being the first to suffer. It did not regain operational status until March 1985, returning to Bagotville, Quebec, fairly soon afterwards.

Attention then shifted to the Sollingen-based and NATO-committed elements of No.1 Canadian Air Group in West Germany where No.439 Squadron had been selected to lead the transition. Unfortunately, No.439 did not begin training until mid-April 1985, almost four months behind schedule. By then, pressure from SACEUR (Supreme Allied Commander Europe) had prompted those responsible for CAF policy to earmark No.409 Squadron for reassignment to Sollingen in order to maintain the desired level of combat readiness. As a consequence, this unit's CF-18s began to reach Europe shortly before the end of May.

Re-equipment of No.439 Squadron occupied most of 1985, this being due to return to Sollingen during December, while the third European-based unit will be No.421 Squadron which apparently disbanded as a CF-104 operator at the beginning of October 1985.

The remaining No.1 CAG Starfighter unit—No.441 Squadron—now looks likely to fill the vacancy left by the departure of No.409 Squadron. Other NORAD-dedicated units which will eventually acquire the CF-18 are Nos.416 and 433 Squadrons. At present, the re-equipment programme is due to be completed in late 1988.

The second overseas customer to opt for the Hornet was Australia. Twin-engined safety, better growth potential and adequate existing avionics

Below: The first Canadian Armed Forces unit to acquire the CF-18 was No.410 "Cougar" Squadron. Normally tasked with crew training duty, it sent a few aircraft to Sollingen, West Germany for familiarisation purposes in 1984, CF-18B 188903 being one of the machines involved.

equipment were the principal factors in this decision. Unlike Canada, however, production of most of the 75 aircraft on order will be undertaken locally by the Government Aircraft Factory.

The first Australian Hornets both came from the McDonnell Douglas line at St Louis and both were two-seat TF-18As, which were employed to train an initial cadre of RAAF pilots in the USA before undertaking a record breaking non-stop 6,672 nautical mile (12,357km) ferry flight from Lemoore to Australia in May 1985. Fabrication of the third Hornet—again a two-seater—was also done at St Louis, and it was shipped to Australia in knock-down kit form for assembly.

All subsequent machines will be manufactured locally. This programme began with TF-18A A21-104 which made its maiden flight on 3 June 1985 and which was delivered on 30 July. Three more TF-18As were due for delivery in 1985, raising the total number on RAAF charge to seven. Production during 1986 will comprise 15 F-18As while 1987 should witness delivery of seven more TF-18As and 11 F-18As, corresponding figures for 1988 being four and 14 respectively. A further 13 F-18As will be handed over to the RAAF during 1989 and production will cease in 1990 with the final four single-seaters.

The first RAAF Hornet operator was No.2 Operational Conversion Unit (OCU) at Williamtown, New South Wales, this having been formed to fulfil the training function in April 1985. With regard to operational elements, No. 75 Squadron is to lead the way at Williamtown where it is due to begin re-equipping in June 1986. Its place in Malaysia will be

Above: A quartet of CF-18As from No.409 "Night Hawk" Squadron fly in formation near Cold Lake, Alberta shortly before being deployed to Sollingen in 1985. Low-visibility unit insignia may be seen near the top of the outer vertical tail surfaces on all four aircraft.

taken by No.79 Squadron which operates Mirages. Following re-equipment, No.75 Squadron will move to Tindal, some 300 miles (483kms) south of Darwin, probably in April 1987.

July 1987 should see re-equipment of No.3 Squadron at Williamtown while No.77 Squadron is to follow suit in April 1988, each of the three operational units being assigned 16 F-18s while the OCU allocation will be 14. From 1988 onwards, part of the fleet will be kept in Malaysia on a rotational basis.

The only other customer is Spain's Ejercito del Aire which originally drew up a requirement for 144 new strike fighters to replace their F-4C Phantoms, Mirage IIIEEs and SF-5 Freedom Fighters. In the event, financial considerations forced a reduction, and Spain ordered 72 aircraft on 31 May 1983 with an additional 12 on option.

Rather confusingly, the Spanish aircraft have been given the designation EF-18 by McDonnell Douglas, the "E" signifying Espana and not an electronic modification. Further confusion looks likely to arise from the fact that the Hornet will be known as the C.15 in Spanish service. All of the 72 aircraft presently on order—comprising 60 single-seat C.15s and 12 two-seat CE.15s—will be built by the parent company and the first example was rolled-out at St Louis on 22 November 1985.

Initial pilot training was to take place in the USA with deliveries being set to commence in June 1986 and initial operating capability in 1987.

6
Colours and Markings

PRODUCTION Hornets feature almost universally drab low-visibility colour schemes, more or less unrelieved by unit insignia. However, most of the prototypes were rather more attractively marked and before discussing colour schemes adopted by production-configured aircraft, it might be worthwhile to examine the prototypes in greater detail.

The very first F-18A (Bu.No.160775) was undoubtedly the most visually pleasing example. It had a very smart basically white finish with blue and gold trim applied to the LEX, wing tips, outer horizontal tail surfaces and leading edges of the vertical tail surfaces. In addition, a blue and gold cheatline also appeared on the fuselage sides, this extending aft from the air intakes to the exhaust nozzles. High visibility red, white and blue national insignia was also carried on the forward fuselage sides, above the port wing and below the starboard wing while the centre fuselage section on both sides of the aircraft

featured the legend "Hornet" in dark blue capital letters.

Other markings applied to Bu.No.160775 comprised Navy titles to port, Marines inscriptions to starboard, a stylized hornet motif on both sides of the nose ahead of the "star-and-bar" national marking and the McDonnell Douglas logo on both outer fin surfaces. All of these were painted in dark blue as was the number "1" which appears on all vertical tail surfaces and on both sides of the nose section, this signifying that the aircraft in question was the first of the FSD batch. The anti-dazzle panel ahead of the cockpit on this aircraft was blue.

Virtually identical markings and colours were also applied to the first TF-18A (Bu.No.160781) which featured the code "T1" on the nose section, alluding to the fact that it was the first two-seater. In common

Below: Operational Hornets are far less visually appealing, as can be graphically seen in this fine in-flight study of an aircraft from VFA-113 "Stingers". Unit insignia is only faintly visible on the outer fin surface.

with the first F-18 and most of the other FSD machines, warning notices such as ejection seat "triangles" and jet intake "chevrons" were in high visibility colours. By October 1982, however, TF-18A Bu.No.160781 had adopted high-visibility red trim on wings, tail surfaces and the LEX as well as the nose modex "150" which almost certainly indicated that it had been reassigned to the Naval Air Test Center's Strike Aircraft Test Directorate. "Navy" and "Marines" titles were also moved aft at this time.

White, with dark blue trim

As far as the other FSD aircraft are concerned, F-18As Nos.2-5, 7 and 8 (Bu.Nos.160776-779, 160782-783 respectively), all began life in a basically white finish with dark blue trim on the LEX, fuselage sides ahead of the air intakes, wing upper and lower

surfaces, horizontal tail surfaces and inner and outer vertical tail surfaces. Anti-dazzle panels were black.

Not surprisingly, subtle variations appeared from time to time, as, for instance, on FSD F-18A No.3 which, in October 1979, had blue and gold trim on the outer part of the horizontal tail, possibly as a result of having "borrowed" this component from the first aircraft. Radome colouring also seems to have varied significantly. Some aircraft (such as Nos.5 and 7) appeared with these in grey while others (notably Nos.4, 6 and 8) employed white radomes. Typically, photographs of No.3 indicate that it used both types at different times.

High visibility national insignia was applied to the same positions as on the first aircraft. These machines also featured dark blue "Navy" and "Marines" inscriptions to port and starboard respectively, these being situated on the rear fuselage rather than below the LEX as was the case with the first F-18A and the first TF-18A. Single-digit FSD numbers—corresponding to the build number—were displayed on the nose section in blue and at the top of the inner and outer vertical tail surfaces in white.

One notable exception to this scheme concerned FSD aircraft No.6 (Bu.No.160780) which was assigned to exploration of the more extreme portions of the flight envelope. Since high visibility was naturally desirable, this wore basically the same pattern as the other FSD Hornets although the blue was replaced by bright red. Apart from this major difference, it appears to have conformed very closely to the other aircraft, displaying dark blue "Navy" and "Marines" titles to port and starboard respectively and with the FSD identification number being presented in blue on the nose and white on the inner and outer fin surfaces. A red and white "candy-striped" nose probe put the final touch to this aircraft's distinctive finish.

The remaining two aircraft from the initial development batch—F-18A No.9 (Bu.No.160785) and TF-18A T2 (Bu.No.160784)—both featured what approximated closely to the eventual production-standard paint job in that they were the first to

appear in low-visibility greys. Both confirmed to previous FSD aircraft practice in displaying "Navy" and "Marines" titles to port and starboard respectively. National insignia appeared in the "low-viz" style above the port wing, below the starboard wing and on both forward fuselage sides below the cockpit. Warning notices were also applied in grey, a rather darker hue being used so as to provide a measure of contrast, while the single-seater also carried the FSD number "9" in grey on the nose section only.

Production colour scheme

Turning to production Hornets, the basic scheme consists of two shades of grey,—or "gray", if you prefer the American style of spelling—the upper surfaces, inner fins and those portions of the fuselage sides not obscured by the wing and horizontal tail surfaces using FS.36375 while the undersides, outer fins and fuselage sides beneath the wings and tail utilize the official colour FS.36495. National insignia, unit markings, fin code letter combinations, nose and tail modex numbers, warning notices and instructions and the anti-dazzle panel ahead of the cockpit employ an even darker and contrasting shade of

Below: Displaying No.410 Squadron's stylised Cougar motif on the top of the fin, a pair of CF-18Bs fly in formation soon after delivery to Canada. Although employing the same basic camouflage pattern as USN/USMC machines, Canadian aircraft are painted in rather darker hues.

grey, this hue having the designation FS.35237.

If such a thing were possible, the Canadian aircraft are even less visually stimulating. Although the basic pattern of application appears to be identical to that of the USN/USMC, the somwhat darker FS.35237 appears on the upper surfaces with FS.36375 on the undersides. Inscriptions, national insignia, unit markings, serial numbers, warning instructions and other notices carried by Canadian F-18s are also displayed in these two shades, FS.36375 being used on the upper surfaces where FS.35237 is the predominant colour and vice versa on the undersides.

With the solitary exception of the Aerospace Engineering Test Establishment (AETE), which uses a dayglo "X" on the fin, such unit markings as have been carried by CAF CF-18s have so far been confined to the top of the outer fin surfaces.

By way of illustration, No.410 Squadron briefly displayed a cougar's head motif on some of its aircraft. Unfortunately, the structural problems encountered with the vertical tail surfaces in late 1984 and early 1985 resulted in a fair degree of interchange of aircraft between units, which culminated in the removal of unit markings and it is not known whether they have been or will be reinstated.

Finally, all of the Canadian machines feature the highly distinctive "false canopy" beneath the nose section. This is intended to confuse an opponent as to aircraft attitude in air combat. Although it appears at first glance to be painted in black, it is actually a very dark grey, the colour reference number possibly being FS.36173.

With regard to other Hornet operators, relatively little information has appeared on the colour scheme to be applied to those aircraft destined for service with Spain's Ejercito del Aire although it appears that it is basically similar to that adopted by Navy and Marine Corps F-18s as well as those of the Royal Australian Air Force.

Thus, RAAF F-18s are painted in two basic shades of grey with a third being employed for notices and instructions. Unusually, however, serial numbers are painted in black while the RAAF aircraft also feature high-visibility national insignia, the familiar "kangaroo" roundel appearing on the nose section beneath the cockpit, with red, white and blue flags being displayed on the outer vertical tail surfaces. The Hornet's large fins do also constitute an admirable "canvas" for colourful unit insignia but so far only the RAAF seems to have taken full advantage of this. As a result, the small number of aircraft presently assigned to No.2 Operational Conversion Unit feature a very smart yellow and black chevron upon which is superimposed a tiger's head.

Below: Employing a mixture of high and low-visibility markings, Australian Hornets are by far the most colourful operational specimens of the type. The aircraft depicted here, TF-18A A21-101, was the first of two two-seaters to be manufactured and test-flown in the USA.

APPENDIX I: HORNET PRODUCTION DATA

US Navy/Marine Corps Aircraft

F-18A		F-18A		F-18A		TF-18A	
160775-780	6	161720-722	3	162420-426	7	161723	
160782-783	2	161724-726	3	162428-477	50	161727	
160785	1	161728-732	5	(probably includes some		161733	
161213-216	4	161734-739	6	TF-18As)		161740	
161248	1	161741-745	5	(Note: Production for		161746	
161250-251	2	161747-761	15	USN/USMC is continuing)		161924	
161353	1	161925-931	7	TF-18A 160781	1	161932	
161358-359	2	161933-937	5	160784	1	161938	
161361-367	7	161939-942	4	161217	1	161943	
161519-528	10	161944-946	3	161249	1	161947	
161702-703	2	161948-987	40	161354-357	4	162402	
161705-706	2	162394-401	8	161360	1	162408	
161708-710	2	162403-407	5	161704	1	162413	
161712-713	2	162409-412	4	161707	1	162419	
161715-718	4	162414-418	5	161711	1	162427	
				161714	1	(Note: Production for	
				161719	1	USN/USMC is continuing)	

EXPORT ORDERS

Australian Aircraft		Canadian Aircraft		Spanish Aircraft	
F-18A A21-1 to A21-57	57	CF-18A 188701-188813	113	F-18A C.15-1 to C.15-60	6
TF-18A A21-101 to A21-118	18	CF-18B 188901-188925	25	TF-18A CE.15-1 to CE.15-12	1

(Note: Spain holds option on an additional 12 aircraft)

APPENDIX II: SPECIFICATION DATA: F-18A VARIANT

Dimensions
Wing span
(less missiles)   37ft 6in (11.43m)
Length   56ft 0in (17.07m)
Height   15ft 3.5in (4.66m)
Tail span   21ft 7.25in (6.58m)
Wheel track   10ft 2.5in (3.11m)
Wing area   400sq ft (37.16 sq m)

Weights
Empty   21,830lb (9,900kg)
Fighter configuration 34,700lb (15,740kg)
Maximum   51,900lb (23,540kg)

Powerplant
Two General Electric F404-GE-400
turbofan engines, each rated at 10,600lb
(4,808kg) thrust dry and 16,000lb
(7,250kg) thrust in afterburner.

Performance
Vmax   Mach 1.
Combat ceiling   50,000ft (15,240m)
Combat radius (VF)   400nm (740km)
Combat radius (VA)   575nm (1,065km)
Ferry range
(unrefuelled)   2,000nm (3,706km)
Initial climb rate 50,000ft/min (254m/sec)
Maximum payload   17,000lb (7,710kg)
        on nine stations

APPENDIX III: HORNET OPERATING UNITS

US NAVY UNITS
Strike Fighter Squadrons (VFA)

Number	Name	Base	Code/CVW	Fleet
VFA-25	Fist of the Fleet	Lemoore, Ca	NK/CVW-14	Pac
VFA-106	Gladiators	Cecil Field, Fl	AD/training	Lant
VFA-113	Stingers	Lemoore, Ca	NK/CVW-14	Pac
VFA-125	Rough Raiders	Lemoore, Ca	NJ/training	Pac
VFA-131	Wildcats	Cecil Field, Fl	AK/CVW-13	Lant
VFA-132	Privateers	Cecil Field, Fl	AK/CVW-13	Lant
VFA-136	Knight Hawks	Cecil Field, Fl	AK/CVW-13	Lant
VFA-137	Kestrels	Cecil Field, Fl	AK/CVW-13	Lant
VFA-192	Golden Dragons	Lemoore, Ca	NE/CVW-2	Pac
VFA-195	Dambusters	Lemoore, Ca	NE/CVW-2	Pac
VFA-303	Golden Hawks	Lemoore, Ca	ND/Reserve	Pac

Test and Other Users

Designation	Name (if applied)	Base	Code
VX-4	Evaluators	Point Mugu, Ca	XF
VX-5	Vampires	China Lake, Ca	XE
NATC (SATD)	—	Patuxent River, Md	7T
NWC	—	China Lake, Ca	—
NTPS	—	Patuxent River, Md	—

US MARINE CORPS UNITS

Number	Name	Base	Code
VMFA-115	Silver Eagles	Beaufort, SC	VE
VMFA-314	Black Knights	El Toro, Ca	VW
VMFA-323	Death Rattlers	El Toro, Ca	WS
VMFA-531	Gray Ghosts	El Toro, Ca	EC

OVERSEAS AIR ARMS

CANADA

Number	Base
409 Sqn	Sollingen, West Germany
410 Sqn	Cold Lake, Alberta
421 Sqn	Sollingen, West Germany (see note)
425 Sqn	Bagotville, Quebec
439 Sqn	Sollingen, West Germany

Note: No.421 Sqn equipped with CF-18 in Canada early in 1986 but returned to West Germany in Summer 1986.

AUSTRALIA

Number	Base
2 OCU	Williamtown, New South Wales
75 Sqn	Williamtown, New South Wales (see note)

Note: No.75 Sqn is due to move to Tindal in April 1987.

SPAIN

The first *Ejercito del Aire* unit to operate the Hornet will be Ala 15 at Zaragoza in 1986.

PRINTED IN BELGIUM BY
proost
INTERNATIONAL BOOK PRODUCTION